NAME THAT TEXT TYPE!

WHAT ARE PLAYS?

Lisa Owings

Property of
Mishawaka-Penn-Harris
Public Library
Mishawaka, Indiana

Lerner Publications Company • Minneapolis

Copyright © 2015 by Lerner Publishing Group, Inc.

All rights reserved. International copyright secured. No part of this book may be reproduced, stored in a retrieval system, or transmitted in any form or by any means—electronic, mechanical, photocopying, recording, or otherwise—without the prior written permission of Lerner Publishing Group, Inc., except for the inclusion of brief quotations in an acknowledged review.

Lerner Publications Company
A division of Lerner Publishing Group, Inc.
241 First Avenue North
Minneapolis, MN 55401 USA

For reading levels and more information, look up this title at www.lernerbooks.com.

All untitled plays copyright © by Lerner Publishing Group, Inc. All rights reserved.

Main body text set in Avenir LT Pro 15/21. Typeface provided by Linotype AG.

Library of Congress Cataloging-in-Publication Data

Owings, Lisa.
　　What are plays? / Lisa Owings.
　　　　pages　cm. — (Name That Text Type!)
　　Includes index.
　　ISBN 978–1–4677–4060–9 (lib. bdg. : alk. paper)
　　ISBN 978–1–4677–4702–8 (eBook)
　　1. Theater—Juvenile literature. I. Title.
PN2037.O95 2015
792.09—dc23   2013046119

Manufactured in the United States of America
1 – BP – 7/15/14

Contents

Introduction: Stories That Come to Life.....4

Setting Up.....6

Telling the Story.....8

Acts, Scenes, and Scripts.....13

From Page to Performance.....16

Types of Plays.....19

Plays Then, Now, and around the World.....23

Now You Do It....29

Glossary....30

Further Information....31

Index....32

Introduction: Stories That Come to Life

Plays are stories that are acted out on a stage. Have you ever seen a play? Maybe you have even been *in* a play!

Plays are exciting to watch. The theater lights dim. Music fills your ears. Then actors come onto the stage. Through their words and actions, they bring a story to life.

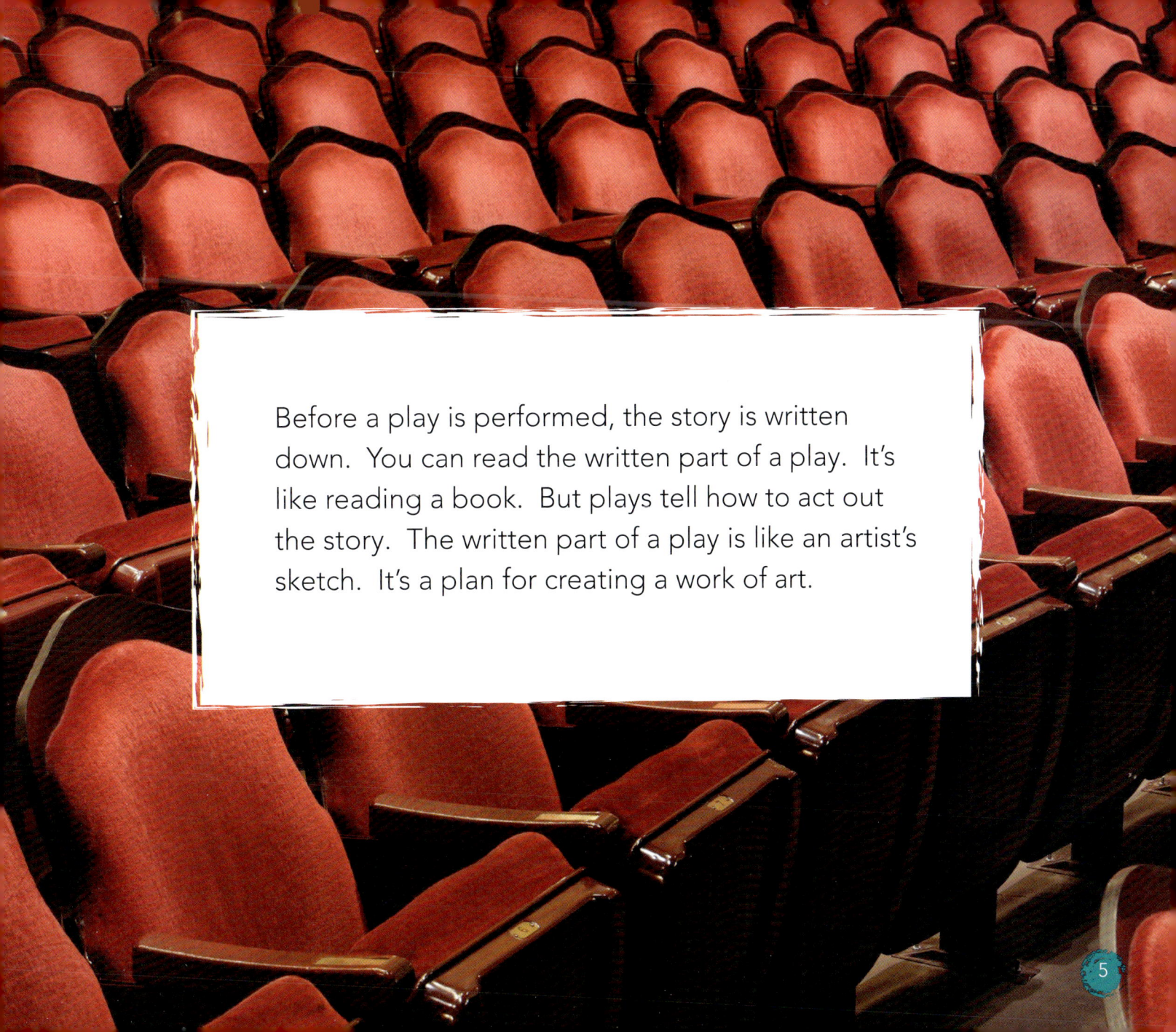

Before a play is performed, the story is written down. You can read the written part of a play. It's like reading a book. But plays tell how to act out the story. The written part of a play is like an artist's sketch. It's a plan for creating a work of art.

SETTING UP

Most plays have the same basic parts. First, a play needs a setting. The audience needs to know when and where the story takes place.

A play also needs interesting characters. The main character is the protagonist. This is the person the audience roots for. The antagonist is the person who tries to mess up the protagonist's plans.

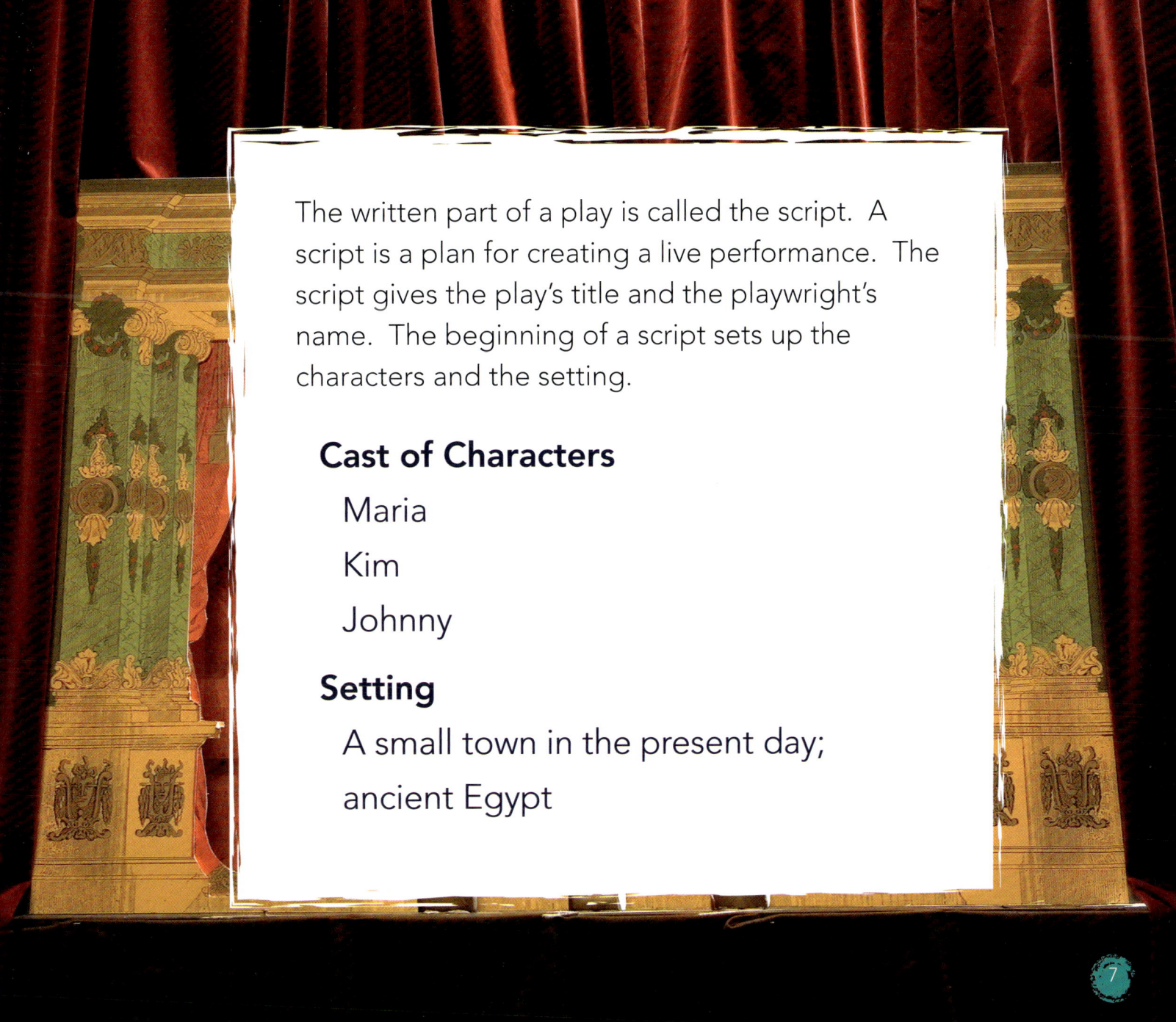

The written part of a play is called the script. A script is a plan for creating a live performance. The script gives the play's title and the playwright's name. The beginning of a script sets up the characters and the setting.

Cast of Characters

Maria

Kim

Johnny

Setting

A small town in the present day; ancient Egypt

TELLING THE STORY

The most important part of a play is the story it tells. A good story has an interesting plot. Each plot has a beginning, a middle, and an end. The beginning introduces the characters and the setting. In the middle, the main characters face challenges. They have to struggle to get what they want. This makes the play exciting.

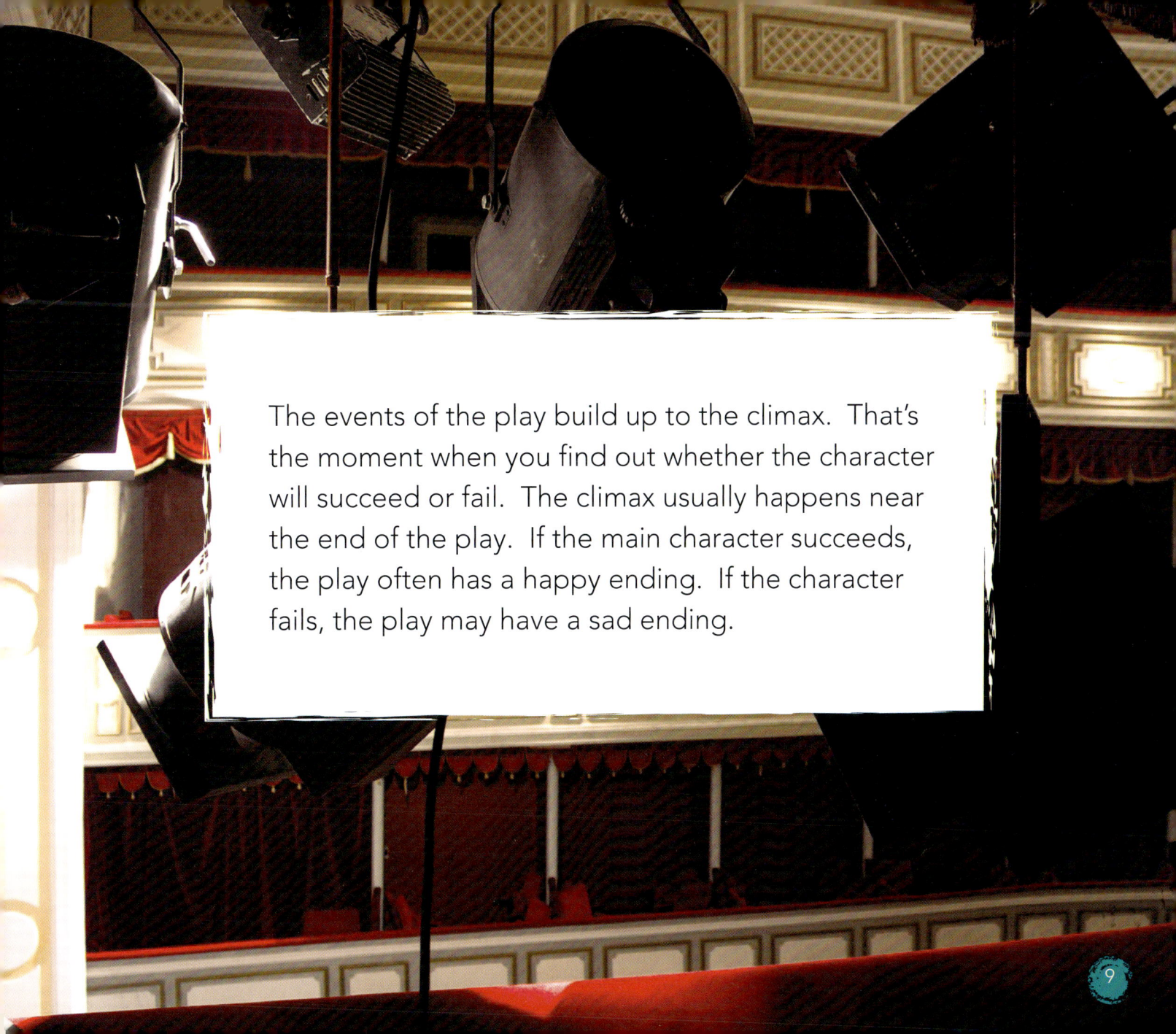

The events of the play build up to the climax. That's the moment when you find out whether the character will succeed or fail. The climax usually happens near the end of the play. If the main character succeeds, the play often has a happy ending. If the character fails, the play may have a sad ending.

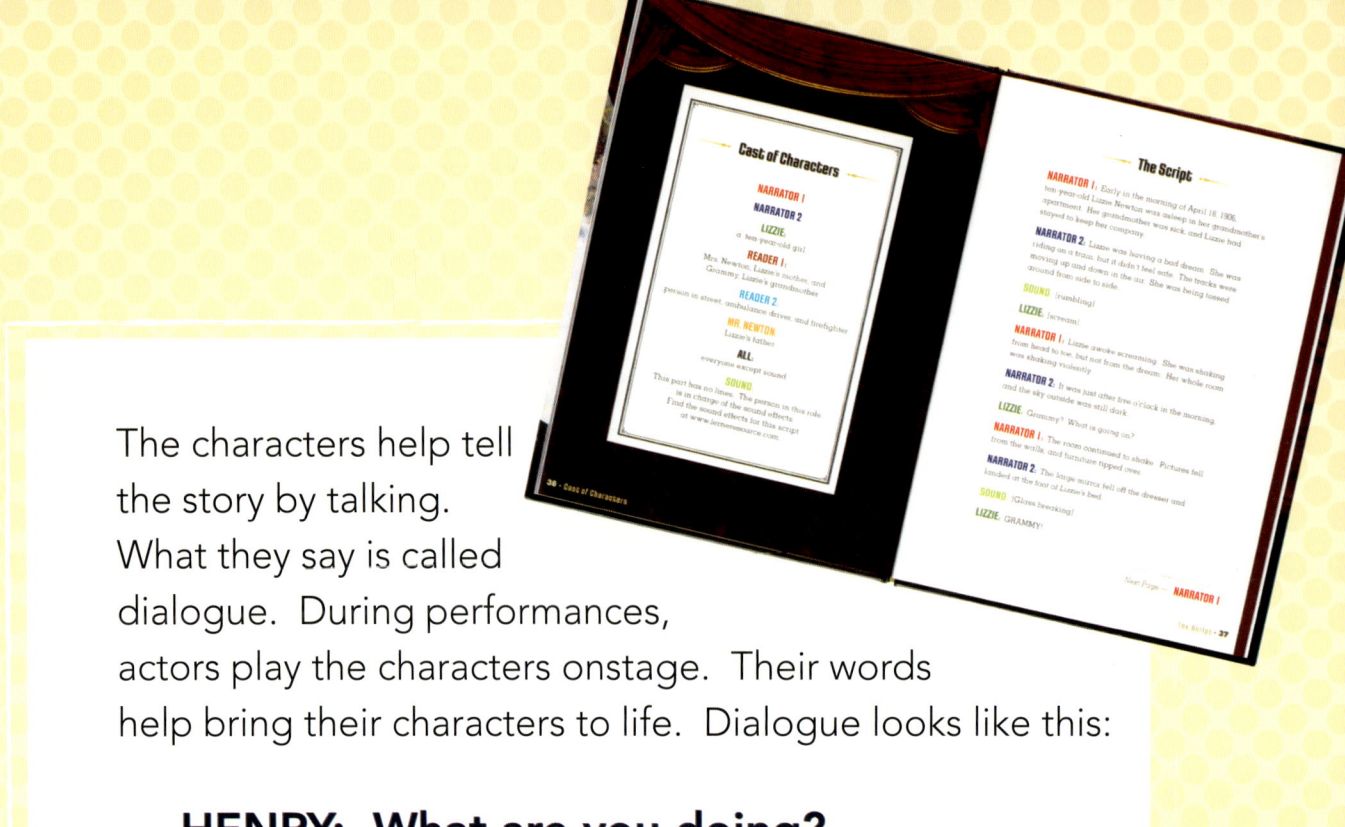

The characters help tell the story by talking. What they say is called dialogue. During performances, actors play the characters onstage. Their words help bring their characters to life. Dialogue looks like this:

HENRY: What are you doing?

JOAN: Oh, nothing much.

The characters' movements also help to tell the story. Stage directions show the actors what to do. When you read a play, stage directions tell you what is happening.

JOAN *is playing in her mother's closet. She finds a small box and opens it. Inside is an old key. She picks up the key. Suddenly, her brother* **HENRY** *enters.*

HENRY: What are you doing?

JOAN: *(hiding the key behind her back)* **Oh, nothing much.**

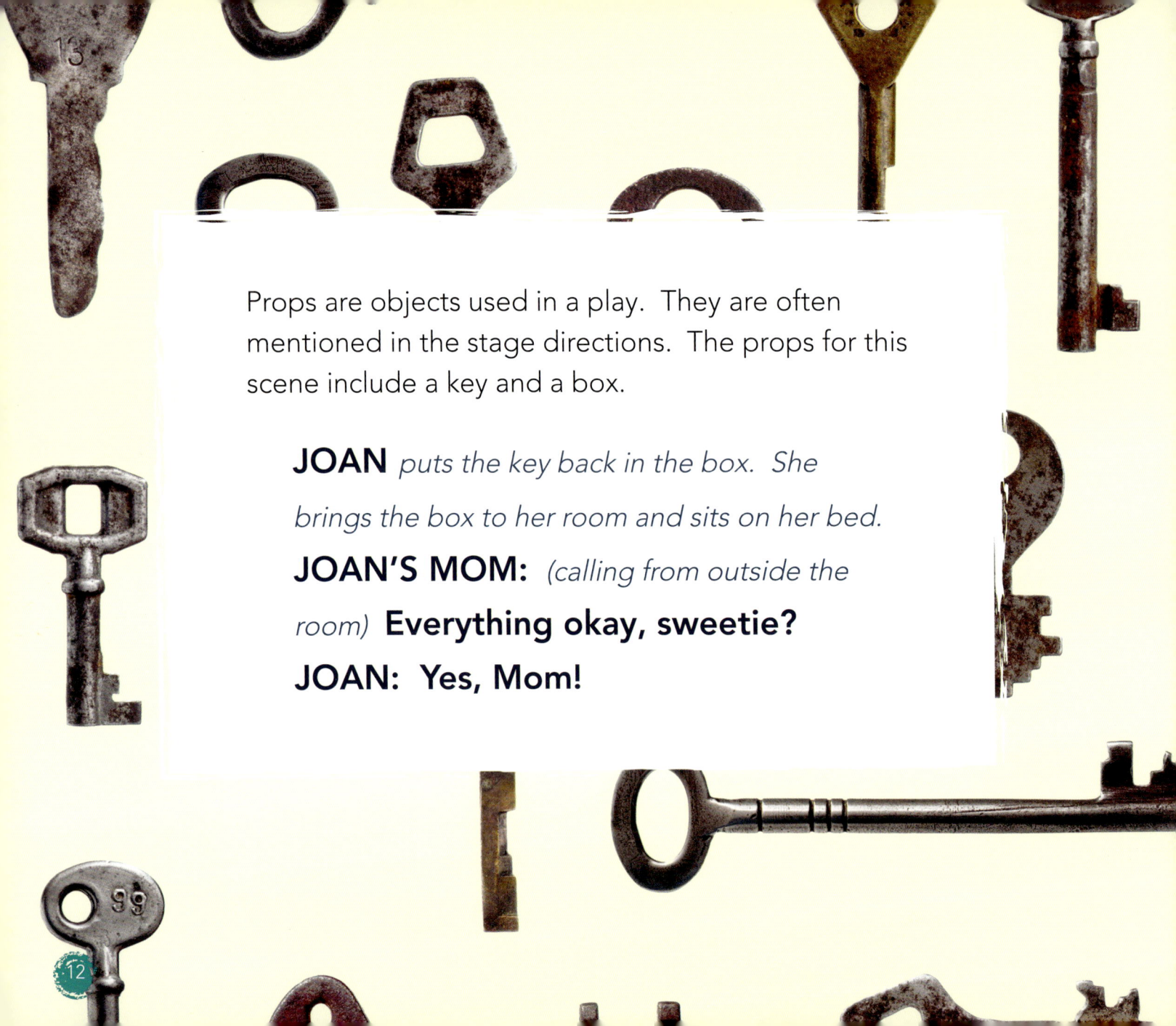

Props are objects used in a play. They are often mentioned in the stage directions. The props for this scene include a key and a box.

JOAN *puts the key back in the box. She brings the box to her room and sits on her bed.*
JOAN'S MOM: *(calling from outside the room)* **Everything okay, sweetie?**
JOAN: Yes, Mom!

ACTS, SCENES, AND SCRIPTS

Plays are divided into smaller parts, like chapters in books. Instead of chapters, plays have acts. Each act is a new part of the story. Many plays have an intermission between acts. This lets the audience take a break.

Each act is divided into smaller parts called scenes. The scene changes when the play moves on to a different time or place. Between scenes, the lights are dimmed. Actors can move without being seen. The setting and props can be changed.

A play's script shows its acts and scenes. The beginning of a scene often explains what's happening.

ACT I

SCENE 2

> **MARIA, KIM,** and **JOHNNY** *are lying on the ground in a pile of sand. They slowly come to their senses. They look around.*

JOHNNY: What happened? Where are we?

KIM: We're in a desert. Duh.

MARIA: Whatever this place is, it's nowhere near home. Look! There are pyramids over there. Like in ancient Egypt! And it's so *hot!*

JOHNNY: Could we . . . could we be dead?

KIM: No, silly. If you were dead, could you feel this? *(She pinches him.)*

JOHNNY: Ow! Quit it, Kim! *(He tries to pinch her back.)*

MARIA: *Enough,* you two! The more important question is, how do we get home?

From Page to Performance

It takes a lot of work to bring a play from the page to the stage. First, a theater has to agree to put on the play. Next, the director studies the play. He or she chooses the cast. The director also decides how the play will be performed. The crew designs the stage to show the setting. They also plan the actors' costumes.

Some crew members practice lighting the stage. They learn when to dim the lights for scene changes. They also use lighting for special effects, such as the storm in this scene:

LIN and **ARI** are walking in the pouring rain. **LIN** leads the way.

ARI: Just admit it, Lin. You have no idea where we are!

LIN: Of course I do! Come on. It's just a little farther.

Suddenly, there's a blinding flash and a crack of thunder. The lights go out.

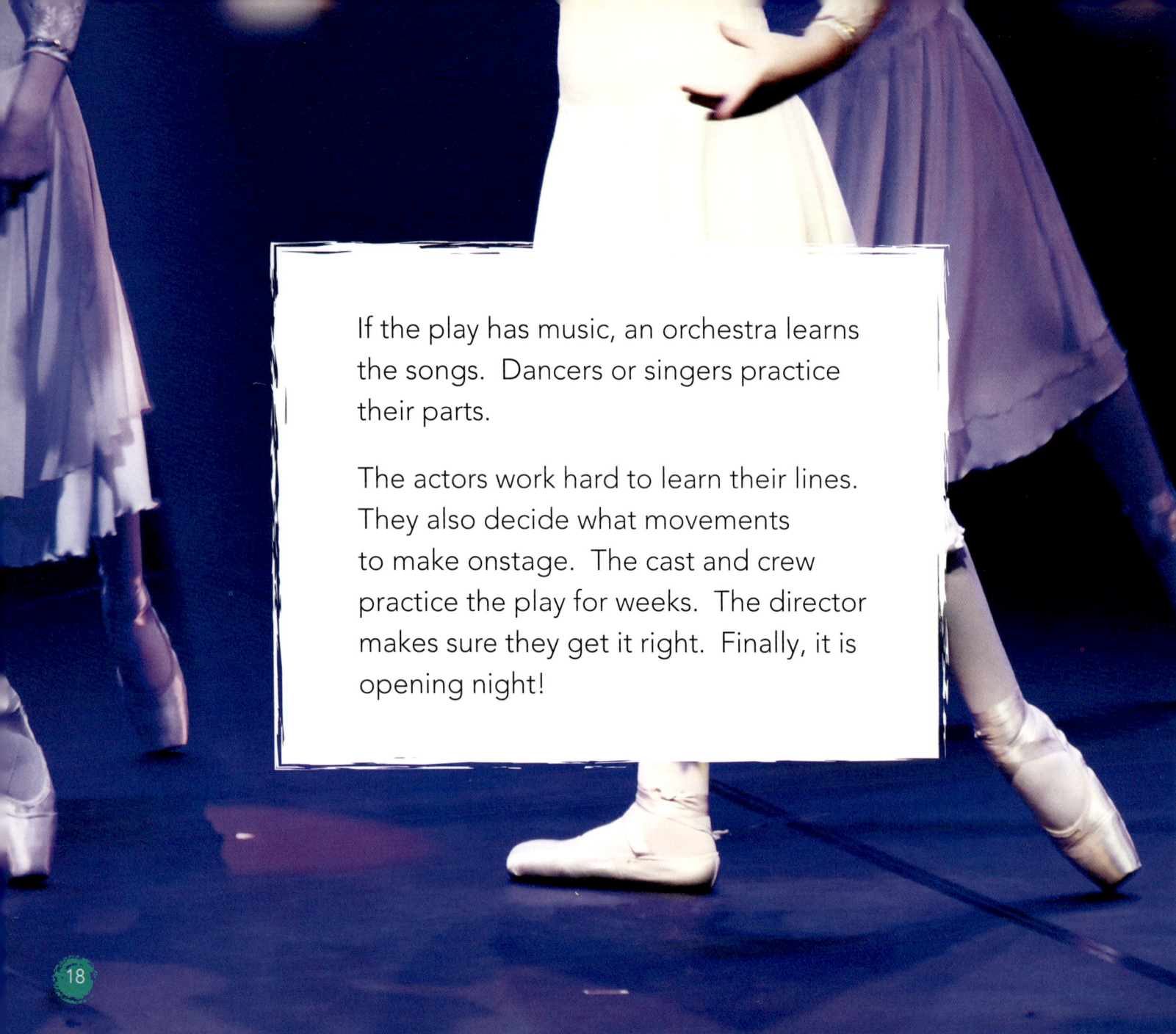

If the play has music, an orchestra learns the songs. Dancers or singers practice their parts.

The actors work hard to learn their lines. They also decide what movements to make onstage. The cast and crew practice the play for weeks. The director makes sure they get it right. Finally, it is opening night!

Types of Plays

Most plays are either tragedies or comedies. Both types began in ancient Greece. Tragedies have unhappy endings. The main characters in most tragedies are heroes. But something bad happens to them in the play. Sometimes the hero even dies.

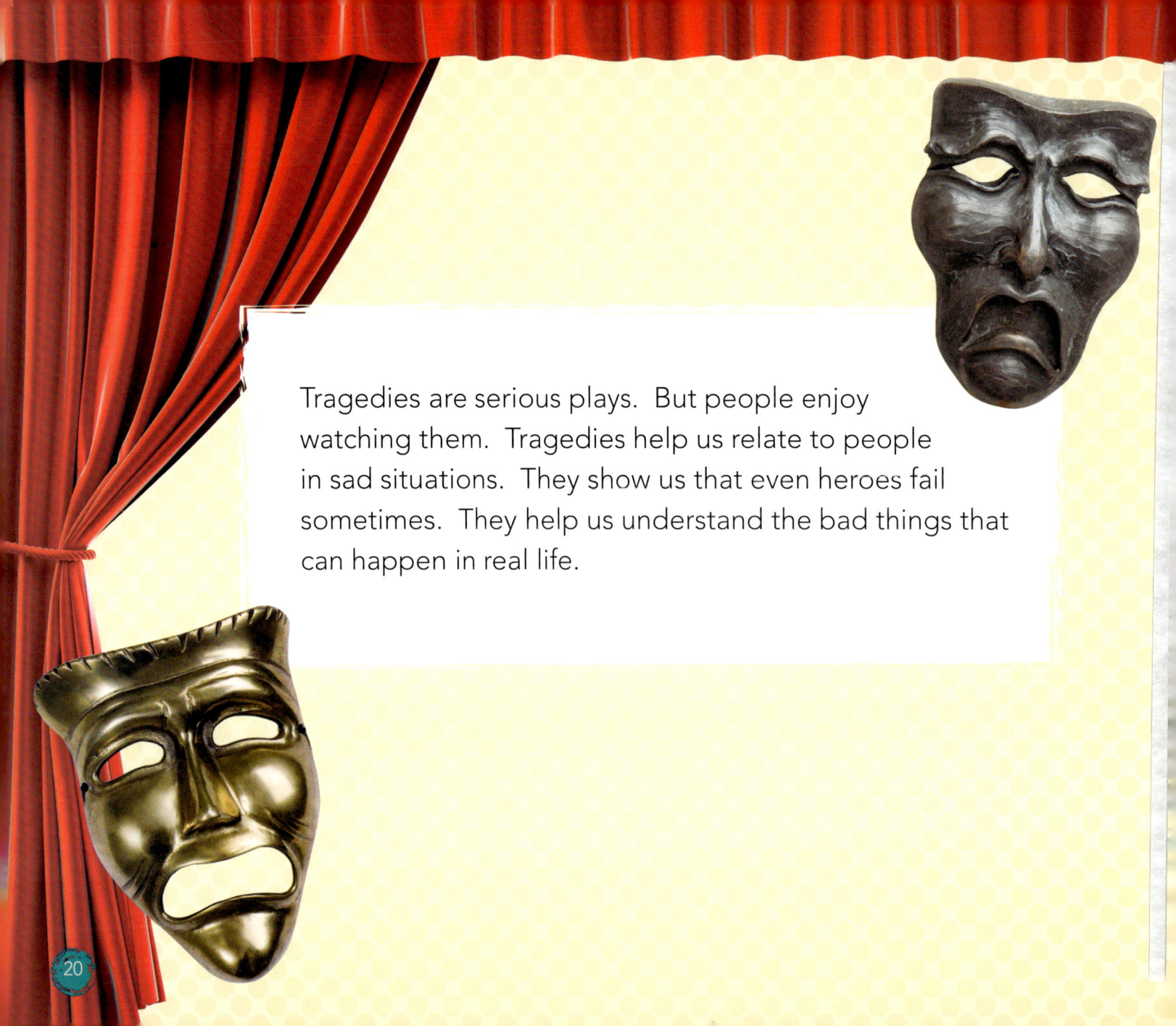

Tragedies are serious plays. But people enjoy watching them. Tragedies help us relate to people in sad situations. They show us that even heroes fail sometimes. They help us understand the bad things that can happen in real life.

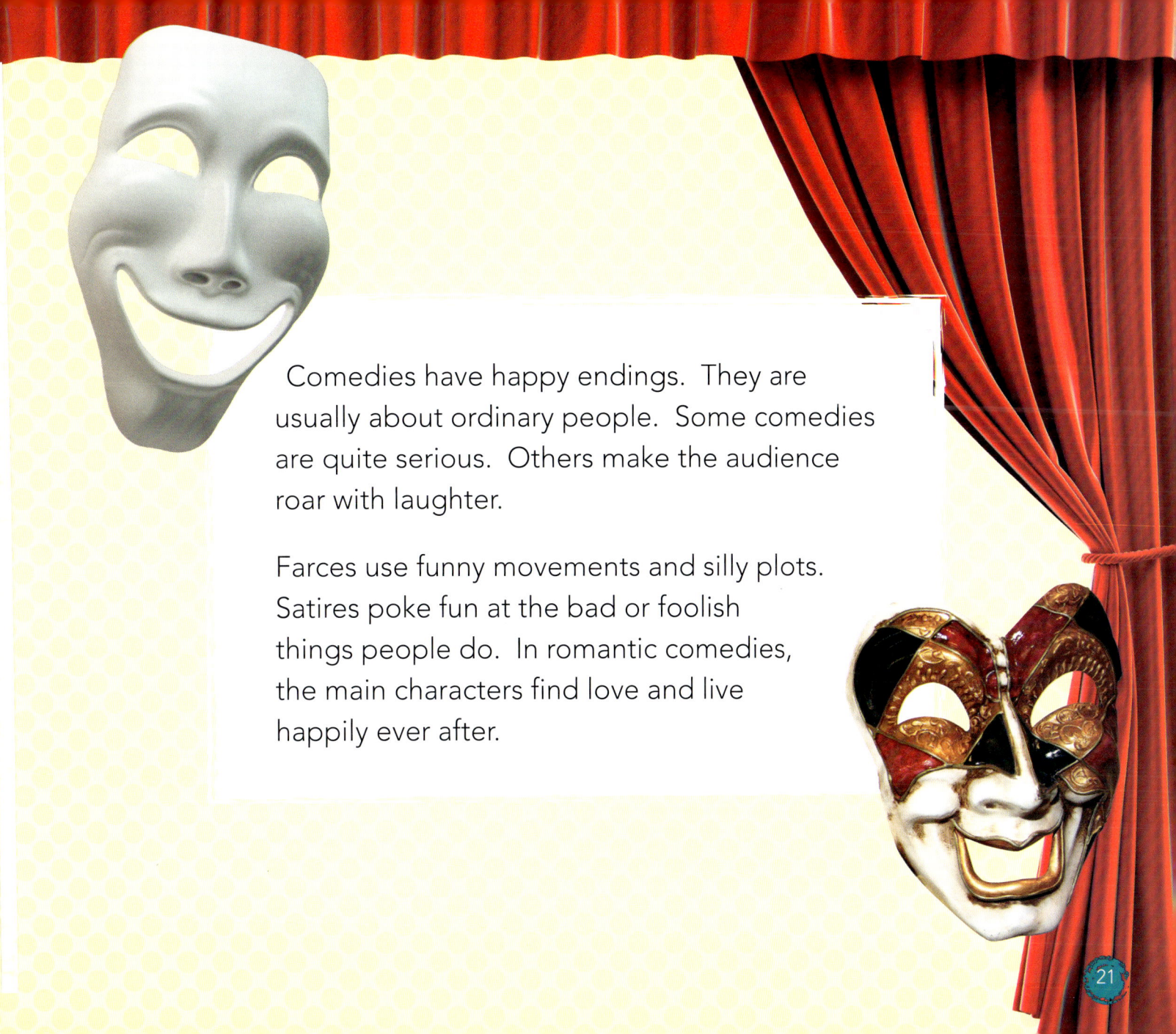

Comedies have happy endings. They are usually about ordinary people. Some comedies are quite serious. Others make the audience roar with laughter.

Farces use funny movements and silly plots. Satires poke fun at the bad or foolish things people do. In romantic comedies, the main characters find love and live happily ever after.

Some plays are not quite tragedies. But they are not quite comedies either. Many people call these plays dramas. Like tragedies, dramas are about unhappy events. But these stories can have happy endings.

Musicals are another type of play. These plays have lots of music and dancing. The songs help tell the story. Most musicals are comedies. But some are dramas or even tragedies.

PLAYS THEN, NOW, AND AROUND THE WORLD

Plays have been part of people's lives for a long time. The first plays were performed in Greece around 500 BCE. Playwrights retold well-known stories of heroes and wars. People gathered in big outdoor spaces to watch the actors. Many ancient Greek plays are still performed.

We still read famous European plays written in the 1500s and the 1600s. English playwright William Shakespeare wrote many plays then. One was the sad story of *Hamlet*. People in this play double-cross one another and fight with swords. *A Midsummer Night's Dream* is a happier play. It tells about magic and fairies.

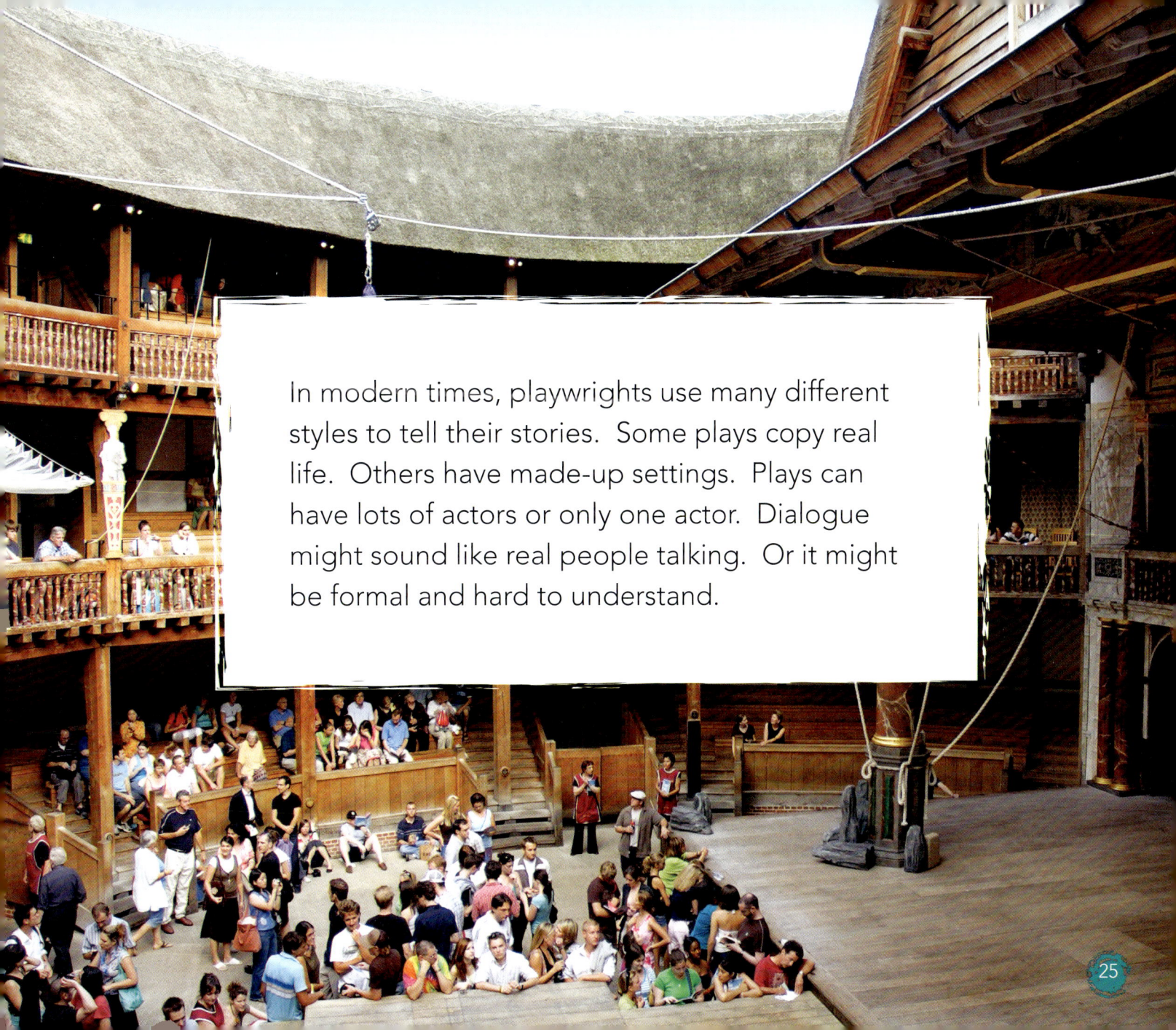

In modern times, playwrights use many different styles to tell their stories. Some plays copy real life. Others have made-up settings. Plays can have lots of actors or only one actor. Dialogue might sound like real people talking. Or it might be formal and hard to understand.

Many Asian plays are centered on music and dance. The first Asian plays were probably performed in India. Kalidasa was a great ancient Indian playwright. His tales always had happy endings.

Chinese plays are usually called Chinese operas. They use songs and dancing to tell a story. The actors wear brightly colored costumes and face paint.

Japan has two major types of plays. Both have music and dancing. Noh plays are familiar stories that follow strict rules. The actors always wear masks. Kabuki plays have fewer rules. They are fun and exciting.

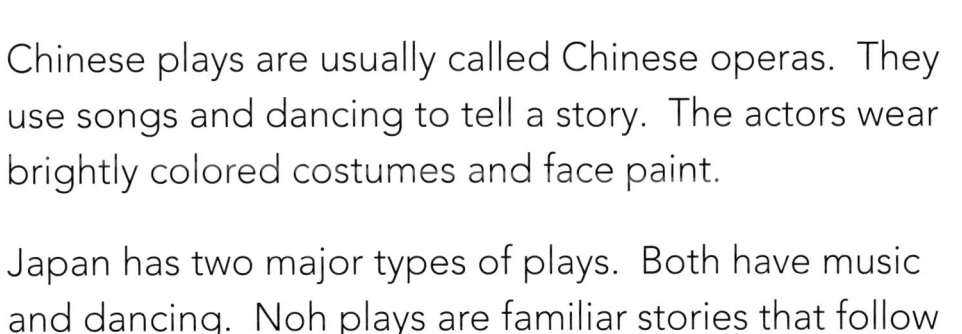

You don't have to go to a theater to enjoy a play. You can read any play you like. When you read plays, you can take your time. You can see exactly what the playwright wrote. It is fun to imagine the characters. Let the stage directions help you picture what happens. When you finish, you can read another play—or write your own!

Now You Do It

You can be a playwright too! First, come up with an idea for a story. Write about a real-life story. Or make something up. A short story works best.

Next, think about the characters. Having fewer characters will make the play easier to perform. Think about the setting. What sets and props could show the setting onstage? Describe the characters and the setting in your script.

Then write dialogue. The dialogue will tell your story. The beginning lets the audience meet your characters. The middle should include a struggle. After the climax, write a happy or a sad ending. Write stage directions to show the actors what to do. What will help your audience understand your story?

Finally, find some friends to help you act out your play. Ask them to read it aloud. What parts can you improve? When you have finished revising, stage a performance!

Glossary

antagonist: a character who tries to stop the hero from reaching his or her goals

cast: the actors in a play

climax: the most exciting or important part of a story. The climax usually happens near the end of a play.

crew: the people who work behind the scenes on a play

dialogue: what characters say to one another

director: the person in charge of putting on a play

intermission: a short break between the acts of a play

playwright: a person who writes plays

plot: what happens in a story

prop: an object that helps show the setting or action of a scene

protagonist: the main character in a story

setting: the place and time in which a story happens

Further Information

Chanda, Justin, ed. *Acting Out: Six One-Act Plays! Six Newbery Stars!* New York: Atheneum Books for Young Readers, 2008.
In this book, you'll find six short plays by beloved children's authors.

Kenney, Karen Latchana. *Cool Scripts & Acting: How to Stage Your Very Own Show.* Edina, MN: Abdo, 2010.
Use the tips in this book to put on your very own play!

Kids Work!
http://www.knowitall.org/kidswork/theater/jobplay/playwright
Use this fun site to learn more about the job of being a playwright.

Perlov, Betty Rosenberg. *Rifka Takes a Bow.* Minneapolis: Kar-Ben Publishing, 2013.
The daughter of two actors discovers the magic of theater in this picture book.

ZOOM Playhouse
http://pbskids.org/zoom/activities/playhouse
Grab your friends and try reading or acting out the short plays on this site.

Expand learning beyond the printed book. Download free, complementary educational resources for this book from our website, www.lerneresource.com.

Index

actors, 4, 10–11, 13, 16, 18, 23, 25, 27

acts, 13–14

characters, 6–7, 8–11, 19, 21, 28

comedies, 19, 21–22

dialogue, 10, 25

dramas, 22

lights, 4, 13, 17

musicals, 22

playwright, 7, 23, 24–25, 26, 28

props, 12–13

scenes, 12, 13–15, 17

script, 7, 14–15

setting, 6–7, 8, 13, 16

stage directions, 11–12, 28

tragedies, 19–20, 22

Photo Acknowledgments

The images in this book are used with the permission of: © Slanapotam/Shutterstock.com, pp. 2, 30, 31, 32; © iStockphoto.com/sitox, p. 4; © iStockphoto.com/BrianBrownImages, p. 5; © Jeff Greenberg/Alamy, p. 6; © imagebroker/Alamy, p. 7; AP Photo/Charles Rex Arbogast, p. 8; © iStockphoto.com/overcrew, p. 9; © Lerner Publishing Group, pp. 10, 13; © AndreaAgrati/iStock/Thinkstock, p. 11; © ultrapor/iStock/Thinkstock, p. 12; © travelshooter/iStock/Thinkstock, p. 14; © iStockphoto.com/cinoby, p. 15; © iStockphoto.com/joeygil, p. 16; © iStockphoto.com/Andrew_C, p. 17; © iStockphoto.com/wsfurlan, p. 18; © iStockphoto.com/essandro0770, p. 19; © Dim Dimich/Shutterstock.com, pp. 20, 21 (curtains); © kps1664/Shutterstock.com, p. 20 (black mask); © Serhiy Kyrychenko/iStock/Thinkstock, p. 20 (gold mask); © Miledy/Shutterstock.com, p. 21 (colorful mask); © Eduard Harkananen/Collection/Thinkstock, p. 21 (white mask); 20th Century Fox/The Kobal Collection, p. 22; © iStockphoto.com/petekarici, p. 23; © Claudio Divizia/iStock/Thinkstock, p. 24; © Bob Masters/Alamy, p. 25; © Yadid Levy/Alamy, p. 26; © Universal Images Group/Alamy, p. 27; © iStockphoto.com/makok, p. 28; © Photoraidz/Shutterstock.com, p. 29.

Front Cover: © Dim Dimich/Shutterstock.com, (curtains), © Lerner Publishing Group, (iPad inset and script), © robert_s/Shutterstock.com, (iPad).